MY SPIR

Ezilausiv

To Bridget,

Thank you & God bless you!

GABRIEL MAYBANK

outskirtspress
DENVER, COLORADO

The opinions expressed in this manuscript are solely the opinions of the author and do not represent the opinions or thoughts of the publisher. The author has represented and warranted full ownership and/or legal right to publish all the materials in this book.

Ezilausiv
My Spiritual Epiphany
All Rights Reserved.
Copyright © 2013 Gabriel Maybank
v2.0, r1.0

Cover Photo © 2013 JupiterImages Corporation. All rights reserved - used with permission.

This book may not be reproduced, transmitted, or stored in whole or in part by any means, including graphic, electronic, or mechanical without the express written consent of the publisher except in the case of brief quotations embodied in critical articles and reviews.

Outskirts Press, Inc.
http://www.outskirtspress.com

ISBN: 978-1-4327-8131-6

Outskirts Press and the "OP" logo are trademarks belonging to Outskirts Press, Inc.

PRINTED IN THE UNITED STATES OF AMERICA

About the Author

Gabriel feels to name himself author would be an incorrect statement and a direct denial of the wisdom bestowed upon him, given the gift of words came from his Lord and Savior Jesus Christ and his Father, the King of kings, God who is above all.

Gabriel was raised in a Christian and military home, and was blessed to travel the world and experience many different cultures.

Gabriel is a Jamaican and African-American poet. He was born in Alexandria, Virginia and now resides in Lawrenceville, Georgia.

Dedicated to:

Angel, Trinity, Adrianna, & Vanessa
The life of my life, soul of my soul, flesh of my flesh,
blood of my blood

My God bless you continually…

"For the word of God is quick, and powerful, and sharper than any two-edged sword, piercing even to the dividing asunder of soul and spirit, and of the joints and marrow, and is a discerner of the thoughts and intents of the heart."

Hebrews 4:12

Special Thanks

I give all thanks and praise to my Father in heaven.
No other praise is as deserving.
To God be the glory on earth as it is in heaven.

Introductory Prayer

Lord,

Please excuse my ignorance, but accept my willingness to learn. My heart desires your Word and my soul desires your Spirit. You've given me a gift in poetry and song with a message. I just want to use them for your will. I don't desire money, but I do desire to be heard. People need to hear and understand the writings and the messages you've given me. If music is how I must reach them, Lord, let me be a musician. If poetry is how I must reach them, Lord, let me be a poet. If ministry is how I must reach them, Lord, let me be a minister. However, you want me to relay these messages let it be: so I won't be lost, my family won't be lost, my children won't be lost; and the people will not be lost. Lord, do not let these gifts be in vain. I'll wait for your answer because you have taught me patience. If it is of you Lord, my simple mind needs a sign it can understand. Not because I lack the faith, but because your will must be done. I don't want to do wrong or venture outside of your grace. You've blessed me and now others must be blessed so your Word may be in them also. Make me a reflection of your light to follow out of these times of darkness.

Amen

Contents

Introduction	i
Chapter 1: Out of the Darkness	1
Good Afternoon Church	3
Bounded	4
Nonchalant	5
Wolf	6
Mind vs. Soul	7
Chapter 2: Vision	9
Lost Vision	12
Lost Vision (part II)	13
When I'm Gone	14
Heaven's Where Home Is	17
What Did You See In Me?	18
Chapter 3: Belief	21
I Am Walking	24
I Can Only Be Me	25
Lil" O Light	26
Move Mountain Move	27
Rain	28
Chapter 4: Love	29
Follow Your Heart	32
Why Did You Come Here?	33
Infatuation	34
The Wise	35
Dear Brother	36
Chapter 5: Forgiveness	37
G.R.I.T.S.	40
Spiritual Simplicity	42

Release Me	43
Forgive Me	44
The Rope	45

Chapter 6: Change — 47

Sometimes	50
The Church	51
The Caterpillar	52
Stable Mind	53
Birth'd in the Grave	54

Chapter 7: Commitment — 55

Generation	58
My Shoes	59
Broken Pieces	60
Blessed	61
Silence	62

Chapter 8: Sacrifice — 63

If I Could Have A Dime	66
Fortunate	67
Old Soul	68
Jericho	69
That's What I Call Pain	70

Chapter 9: Obedience — 71

Silent Weapon	74
Flaws	75
Exodus	76
Ignorance	77
Humbled	78

Chapter 10: Works — 79

Israel Me	82
Regard	83
Tap, Tap, Tap!	84

The Ways of Man	86
Job Fair	87

Chapter 11: Into The Light — 89
- Sky Music — 91
- I Am the Night — 92
- Mind vs. Soul (Part II) — 93
- Confusion — 94
- Wisdom — 95

Conclusion — 97
- Concluding Prayer — 99

Appendix — 101

Study Material — 105
- Foreigners on Earth — 106
- Staying Put — 108
- Army of God: Part I — 110
- Army of God: Part II: Desert Training — 113
- Growing Your Seed — 116

Introduction

"When I open my mouth, everything desolate and vile has the opportunity to come out. But when I open my heart, only my spirit can speak, having the Spirit of Christ - it speaks the most beautiful language of all."

- Gabriel Maybank -

"Ezilausiv" means visualize your reflection because it is the reflection of the word visualize. Please use this book as a personal guide for your own spiritual growth. It was only from my own personal experiences and my growing relationship with the Lord, that I present this vision and these poems to you.

Chapter 1

Out of the Darkness

"But ye are a chosen generation, a royal priesthood, an holy nation, a peculiar people; that ye should show forth praises of him, who hath called you out of darkness into his marvelous light;"

I Peter 2:9

"Out of the Darkness," simply means taking the blindfold off our eyes that stops us from seeing God's will. When you live in darkness, you need a light to see your way out. This book is a reflection of God's light, through me, showing you a way out. A way out of the sin that threatens to keep you bound.

Sin is the love of the things of this world, an offense or revolt against God, deliberate defiance, wickedness, iniquity, and ungodliness. "For all that is in the world, the lust of the flesh, and the lust of the eyes, and the pride of life..." (I John 2:16) The world breeds jealousy, pride, lust, greed, and death. Sin is darkness. Sin is foolishness and unwise. If you are controlled by the things of this world you are in sin, thus in bondage.

Some people search for freedom here on earth. Our time on earth is but a flash of lightning compared to a time in eternity. I'd rather have my freedom for eternity than for a short while here on earth. If you are in the light then you don't have to be bound in either life.

Come out from your evil ways and simple human understandings and explore the mind of God. God's wisdom surpasses all that we could ever think. He is the maker and creator of our souls. Who then shall we follow here on earth? "...Behold, the fear of the Lord, that is wisdom; and to depart from evil is understanding." (Job 28:28)

How long will you entertain evil thoughts knowing that your judgment could come at any moment? You should feel as though an angel is in heaven right now pleading your case, that God should not judge you this instant. "Then he is gracious unto him, and saith, ...Deliver him from going down to the pit: I have found a ransom." (Job 33:24)

Good Afternoon Church

Good afternoon church, May I speak for a minute?
God's in my heart and pressing hard on my spirit.
My mind says be quiet but my mouth won't listen.
You need to hear the word that my God is delivering.

Good afternoon church, I know I only said a minute.
I've been going through some things
And wondering if God has been in it.
'Cuz I never felt a love so strong, that even when I'm wrong
He puts his hand upon my shoulder and says "Come on."

Yea though I walk through the valley
How could I move mountains walking through these dark alleys?
But if you think about it that's where they are.
I'm searching for the light at the end of the tunnel
And your water I yearn for.

Life is not promised and death is trying to find me.
Free my spirit Lord because these demons are trying to
Bind me and blind me.

But I don't see it with my own eyes
Or walk with my own feet, You show me.
Every time I think I'm going to fall you hold me.
Fire is burning at my toes.
Struggle is a life-long battle even when you get old.
A lot of things are unknown,
But in God we trust.
Almighty Alpha and Omega God lives in us.
God lives in us.

August 21, 2007

Bounded

...to be free as the wind
I could go where I wanna go
Fly as high as I wanna fly
...but to where?

...to flow as the river
I could be calm and cool as the morning
Rush straight into a wide-open sea
...then what am I?

...to shine as the light
I could travel for miles into uncharted territory
Visit places never before seen to man
...until the darkness

Even the sun doesn't shine everywhere at once.

April 4, 2009

Nonchalant

Sound does not care
    Whose mind it enters.
Wind does not care
    Whose skin it touches.
Dust does not care
    Whose blood it swallows.
Sin does not care
Whose soul it follows.

                        April 2. 2009

Wolf

A wolf is lurking in the shadows, so beware.
Angels are encamped around you, don't be scared.
If you're surrounded by an army, then there must be an attack.
They're watching your every move, see a wolf hunts in a pack.

Beware, Beware!

Their footsteps are very near
They'd rather you know they were there,
Just to instill fear.

Beware, Beware!

Lust is in your workplace,
Luring you to bed.
Watch her deceitful eyes
She's the first to attack your head.

Anger is no stranger, if you keep letting him in.
He's the type that never leaves
He destroys all he's given.

Doubt is at your window, showing you the impossible.
Pay him no attention; because God is not that optional.
Look out for pride, he runs ahead in front of you.
Waiting to trip you up at your greatest moment and pummel you.

Greed follows behind you, picking up on your scent.
Signaling to all the others, where you go and where you went.
Beware, Beware!

For the alpha wolf is sin.
He's lurking in the shadows waiting to strike you dead.

April 10, 2009

Mind vs. Soul

Shut up I say…Shut up I said!
Why are you screaming?
Ha!
You thought someone was listening?
They can't even hear you…
I can barely hear you.
Speak up!
Go ahead and yell then.
Look, they ain't even paying you no attention.
Not even one of them.
Did you hear me?
NOT EVEN ONE!
Ha Ha Ha!
You make me laugh.
You're so pathetic,
Matter fact you make me sick.
My stomach turns every time I hear your voice.
They all feel the same way too…

Shut up I say…Shut up I said!
You make me so mad with all that racquet
La la la la la I can't hear you.
Hey!
Do you mind?
I'm trying to go to sleep.
Can you please- STOP!
For real!
I can't take it anymore.
I have a headache.
Are you going to do this all day and all night?
Once again, they…are…not…listening!!!
THEY ARE NOT LISTENING!!!
I'm starting to think you're not even listening.

Hello!?
Can you hear me?
Knock, knock, knock…come on man…

Shut up I say…Shut up I said!
Okay…okay
I'll hear you out.
Wait!?
I don't have to listen to anything you say
I'm in control here.
I don't even know what you're saying.
What? You bilingual now?
What does that mean anyway?
Look, I'm trying to talk to you but all you do is scream.
You act like you're in jail or something.
Hey!
Calm down, you're stressing me out.
I can't think straight with you yelling all the time.
What in the world does "FREEDOM" mean anyway?

Shut up I say…Shut up I said!
FREEDOM! FREEDOM! FREEDOM!
My soul screams FREEDOM!

       January 1, 2009

Chapter 2

Vision

"Where there is no vision the people perish: but he that keepeth the law, happy is he."

Proverbs 29:18

"Now I am come to make thee understand what shall befall thy people in the latter days: for yet the vision is for many days." (Daniel 10:14)

To even begin to understand the Word of God and its purpose, you must realize there is a spiritual realm. In the spiritual realm, there is a division between good and bad or righteousness and evil. God is the Light, the head of all righteousness, and Satan, the prince of this world, is evil and lies in the shadow of darkness. It is also important to know that there is a spiritual conflict, or battle between the two involving the souls of human beings. The Lord wants you to be in the light; the light is knowledge and knowledge saves. Satan wants you to be in darkness; darkness is sin and sin kills.

"The fear of the Lord is the beginning of knowledge: but fools despise wisdom and instruction." (Proverbs 1:7) To be able to fear the Lord you would have to believe that he exists. Fear leads to obedience, obedience to understanding, and understanding to love. Satan desires the same thing but his ways are evil and result in death. The result of fearing the Lord is eternal life, but most people fear death instead of fearing life. The fear of death causes people to want to gain everything in this life: money, power, respect. But, if you are in the 'know', you would fear what is to come in your eternal life and the things of this world would not have much value to you. "For where your treasure is, there will your heart be also." (Matthew 6:21)

Why is it important to choose and follow the Lord? Well, if you fear death now, how much worse will your death be eternally by not following the Lord? Jesus has given us the promise of life eternally with his Father, which is God. God's wisdom is above all wisdom; he is the creator of all things. Why not follow His Word? Some things cannot be explained unless he chooses to reveal it to us. But through the Word that we have now, which is the Holy Bible, we know what was and what is to come. We may not know exact dates or facts, but what we do know is he has given us the Word and the Word saves. "The light of the body is the eye: if therefore thine eye be single, thy whole body shall be full of light. But if thine eye be evil, thy whole body shall be full of darkness. If therefore the light that is in thee be darkness, how great is that darkness! (Matthew 6:22-23)

I started this book in December 2008, I believe. It was supposed to be a book of poems on the blindness of people. People who seemed like they couldn't see the corruption of the government, the music, and other things like television. Things that frustrated me about the nation we live in: and how people are worshipping money, wealth, and possessions, relating happiness to having things, and how they constantly fill our minds with things we don't need, and make us want and want more. They took the music and all the other things in which people try to concentrate on to just enjoy life and put prices on them. Even simple things in our lives involve money. God must have felt my passion but had a different vision in mind.

As I started looking over my poems after about a month of writing, I realized they were becoming a lot more religious. Soon after, God gave me a title, a format, the chapters and all the words. All I had to do was write them down. The more I wrote the more I began to understand what was really happening. The real battle was spiritual and you could see the changes in people all over world.

The more I read in the Bible, the more things made sense. Scriptures like, "For the love of money is the root of all evil..." (I Timothy 6:10) and "This know also, that in the last days perilous times shall come. For men shall be lovers of their own selves, covetous, boasters, proud, blasphemers, disobedient to parents, unthankful, unholy, Without natural affection, trucebreakers, false accusers, incontinent, fierce, despisers of those that are good, traitors, heady, high-minded, lovers of pleasures more than lovers of God; having a form of godliness, but denying the power thererof: from such turn away. For of this sort are they which creep into houses, and lead captive silly women laden with sins, led away with divers lust, ever learning and never able to come to the knowledge of truth." (II Timothy 3:1-7) These things are taking place today and people don't even realize it. So the Lord said, "Show them."

Lost Vision

Realize the vision; visualize the division.
Separate mind and body to conquer Satan's retention.
Regenerate the religion to God given precision.
Those lost along the way, fallen souls negate redemption.
Of love and fear, whom gets both, regains dominion.
A house up on the rock avoids sinful submission.
Soft as a whisper, listen; when he calls be in position.
Just a graceful decision determines if we're forgiven.
Earth is no comprehension for spiritual intervention.
From dust to dust your sin and skin is the remission.
Ain't no heavenly pension you can save so pay attention.
Pray that you venture up on your next terrestrial mission.
Earth is no comprehension for spiritual intervention.
Realize the vision; visualize the division.
Ain't no heavenly pension you can save so *pay* attention.
And pray that you venture up on your next terrestrial mission.

February 16, 2009

Lost Vision (part II)

Wake up and smell the coffee,
Every morning to keep them demons up off me
I say a word to the Father to watch me
And to give me the strength consciously not to be tempted constantly
Use all that is given to the fullest extent properly
Yes I'm God's property, to the world microscopic see
But under the light of the Spirit I'm reborn a much larger be
    -ing, seeing it all through reality
Up out of the shadows of darkness now I speak factiously
Viciously into the heart, mind, and memories
Stardust is followed by a man's lust to wanna be
But your creation was designed before you were a seed conceived
And your repentance is required before you can be a soul received
Don't follow me, follow the Word and the prophesies
He ain't died on the cross so we can be lost, believe

                    March 5, 2009

When I'm Gone

Who knows when, who knows who?
What if it's me, what if it's you?
How will it be and what will I do?
When the Lord comes calling! When the Lord comes calling!

It's been a long road, but is this the end, I don't know?
When it looks near I'm back on it again.
Will I have time to tell my family and friends?
You'll have plenty of time for that when the surgery is finished.

I can't win for losing and I'm losing to win,
Changing CD's, and then I'm in the back of a sedan
With my hood rolled up like a burrito.
How'd I walk away from that? The Lord was in the front seat holmes!
And if he wasn't then who knows?
Will life go on if blood is leaking from my head down to my toes?
And I'm wondering can he save me?
But in the blink of an eye I'm gone and my mama lost her first baby.

Survived a close one, too many times been close son.
I need to change before my open book becomes a closed one,
And they read off the last chapter.
That's why I'm trying to do something now.
Who knows what happens after
When I'm gone…

Who knows when, who knows who?
What if it's me, what if it's you?
How will it be and what will I do?
When the Lord comes calling! When the Lord comes calling!

Will it be during the day or dead in the night,
On an empty road by myself right after the light?

Will I even have the chance to think fight or flight,
With a telephone pole on the roof and I'm inside?

Drunkenness kills other people but I'm hurting myself.
Still I'm sober enough to get out the car and go call for help.
The Lord must have been in the liquor, every time I took a sip.
No explanation why he don't want my spirit.
I know he's calling me, but I don't seem to hear it.

Steady saying help me please and he steady show appearances, I know.
On the curb and in handcuffs,
Instead of in a pine-box somewhere in a sandlot.
With a stone on my head and a cold date,

It got to be a reason why he keeps me in this place safe,
Safe enough for them to read the next chapter.
That's why I'm trying to do something now.
Who knows what happens after
When I'm gone…

Who knows when, who knows who?
What if it's me, what if it's you?
How will it be and what will I do?
When the Lord comes calling! When the Lord comes calling!

Will he take me in my sleep lying next to 40 people,
And nobody even knows, they got no clue that I'm deceased?
Never realized when I put my head down I would rest in peace.
Not even see another sunny day or kick it with my peeps.

Never smoke another blunt a weed or drink another brew.
And I never got to drop a seed or see how much my sisters grew.
Who knew, that at lights out that my lights out and its nothing I could do
And this time- the Lord is calling for me and not for you?

Shed no tears and show no fear because I knew this day would come.
And there's no point to run because it's coming quick just like a gun.
When it blast, and now I'm just the past.
Couldn't tell you when for certain 'cuz tonight could be my last.

Looking forward to tomorrow hopefully I get to see it.
No matter what I'm going through at least I know I'm breathing,
Long enough for them to read another chapter.
That's why I'm trying to do something now.
Who knows what happens after
When I'm gone…

        June 3, 2007

Heaven's Where Home Is

It's safe to say…
Heaven's my home so I guess I'm homeless
Looking for the light and don't know where the road is
Searching for the truth but it's lies they told us
Trying to find the way like nomadic explorers

Meda ahora,
We're looking for change now
The cross around your neck doesn't mean that you're saved now
This is the devil's playground and we're all in the sandbox
Needing help out and he already had his hand out

It's safe to say…
We're living wrong headed right for destruction
Got to save my soul from spontaneous combustion
Things going bad find a church to rush in
Rush out just as fast when they start back working

Lurking in the shadows- awaiting your down fall
One set of footprints so I can stand tall
Call me home and hope he recognize my face
Hand me my wings open up the heavenly gates
It's safe to say…

Heaven's where home is…

2005

What Did You See In Me?

What did you see in me?
 ...that I can't see in my self
 You looked down that dusty road and noticed me upon the shelf.
 All these years you've waited patiently just to call my name.
 On top of that, you've waited longer just for me to do the same.

What did you see in me?
 ...when all my dreams and hopes have failed
 You gave me everything I needed for the journey you've prepared.
 Every experience of defeat was another lesson learned.
 Every battle that I conquer shows me how much grace I've earned.

What did you see in me?
 ...at times I felt so brittle and weak
  Thru my faith you make me stronger than lion's paws and eagle's beaks.
I'm surrounded by your angels they protect and fight for me.
 How could I deserve a warrior whom has stood before the king?

What did you see in me?
 ...that made my soul a place for you to dwell
 You looked down that dusty road and noticed me upon the shelf.
  Before you even wore the crown, you thought of me and no one else.
 You looked down that dusty road and noticed me upon the shelf.

What did you see in me?
    …that made you say, "Wait!" "Right there" "Yea him"
    You knew me by my heart before I even grew one limb.
    Then you made me not forget you like I've known you once before.
    The cross is a reminder how to get to you once more.

What did you see in me?
    …that you drew me to you
    Can great wisdom and great power have a purpose for a fool?
    You're the Alpha and Omega, the Beginning and the End.
    Yet, you give me talents so somewhere I can fit in

What did you see in me?
    …that you would look past all my sins
    And forgive all of the wrong, love me, and be a friend.
    Could you not find anyone else perhaps more holier, more worthy?
    Like a pastor or a priest, someone righteous, more deserving.

What did you see in me?
    …that I can't see in myself
    You looked down that dusty road and noticed me upon the shelf
    Before you even wore the crown, you thought of me and no one else.
    You looked down that dusty road and noticed me upon the shelf.

March 24, 2009
R.I.P. Chief

Chapter 3

Belief

"But without faith it is impossible to please him: for he that cometh to God must believe that he is, and that he is a rewarder of them that diligently seek him."

Hebrews 11:6

"In the beginning was the Word, and the Word was with God, and the Word was God. The same was in the beginning with God. All things were made by him; and without him was not any thing made that was made. In him was life; and the life was the light of men. And the light shineth in darkness; and the darkness comprehended it not." (John 1:1-5) The Word is the Light and the Light is wisdom, and understanding, and knowing God. To know God is to believe that He is and gain wisdom and understanding through the Word; to know the Word is to know God.

Believing is a continuous battle of the flesh and the spirit. "Now faith is the substance of things hoped for, the evidence of things not seen." (Hebrews 11:1) Faith requires that we see with the heart of our spirit and believe. The flesh requires that we see with our natural eyes and believe. "For we walk by faith, not by sight:" (II Corinthians 5:7) Faith comes from the Word of God, the 'Light', and the flesh does not understand believing in something intangible. God creates by the Word, commands by the Word, and judges by the Word. "So then faith cometh by hearing, and hearing by the word of God." (Romans 10:17)

Now the ultimate question, what do I believe in and why? "…The word is nigh thee, even in thy mouth, and in thy heart: that is, the word of faith, which we preach; That if thou shalt confess with thy mouth the Lord Jesus, and shalt believe in thine heart that God hath raised him from the dead, thou shalt be saved. For with the heart man believeth unto righteousness; and with the mouth confession is made unto salvation." (Romans 10:8-10) If you believe that, God has given you the opportunity to put his Word in you. Salvation produces wisdom and wisdom produces truth. "God is a Spirit: and they that worship him must worship him in spirit and in truth." (John 4:24)

God is also the truth. Knowing the truth frees your spirit. Sin bounds your spirit and blinds you from the truth, or 'the Light'. The world is sin in a spiritual sense. "He that commits sin is of the devil; for the devil sinned from the beginning. For this purpose the Son of God was manifested, that he might destroy the works of the devil." (I John 3:8) God does not want us to be judged guilty. He does not want to punish us for our sins, he'd rather we believe in him and follow his Word. There is nothing to gain by following the ways of the world but death. "For God so loved the world, that he gave his only begotten Son, that whosoever believeth in him should not perish, but have everlasting life." (John 3:16)

I had a discussion with a man, who was a Rastafarian, about the differences in our religion. Every time I would ask him what he believes, he would say, "I don't believe, I know". I wasn't trying to convert him or anything I was just curious about why he chose to be a Rasta. I left the conversation angry because I wasn't able to explain to him, the way I wanted to, the reason for my belief. What he said, "I don't believe, I know", just kept ringing in my head the rest of that day through the next. How does he "know", what makes him so sure, and to know is to believe, right? I kept comparing the differences and trying to figure out if he could have been right or not, or if I was right or not. To be honest, it gave me quite a headache.

After tedious studying and trying to learn the whole Bible in one day, I got it. Something clicked in my head that made me realize why I felt so strongly about what he said. It also made me realize there was a purpose for that conversation and it wasn't to learn another practice or question my own. It was an example of how I should be with my own belief. It was then I realized I also "know". It might not have come out then because it wasn't the time or the place, but God was just showing me because I believe in my heart that I already know him and he knows me.

I Am Walking

I am walking…
My feet do not move.
I may even run,
My legs have no motion.
My arms swing front to back,
But my shoulders are still.
Light shines in every angle of my path,
I can't see where I am going.
Darkness follows behind me,
I've seen where I've been.
I am walking…
But I am walking by faith.

December 21, 2008

I Can Only Be Me

You look into my eyes and what do you see?
A quiet and timid person is what you perceive.
But if you look a little closer, go deep within.
You'll see the person that lies within.
And what you see may blow you away.
Because this person inside me has more power and will,
Than you can ever comprehend!

                        Written By: Tiffany Maybank
                              December 21, 2008

Lil" O Light

I looked out into the wind and fierce roars of thunder as a
    Lion prowling in the jungle.
Beyond the falls of teardrops that slammed the concrete and
    The shabby aluminum roof that was over my head,
    Which could fall any minute.
There…in the distance, was a lil' o light flickering as if it were
    Jumping up and down calling my name.
"Over here! Over here!"
Couldn't tell how far it was or if there was any shelter nearby.
"Is anybody there?" I called out.
But a pop of lightning quieted my screams.
I looked down at my busted old kicks and jeans that were old as me.
My over-worked t-shirt and jacket weren't much either.
Venturing all the way out there in this storm
    Where the giant fist of water blackened the eyes of the street…
Nope… not for me.
But that light…that lil' o light was still flickering.
Could it be a place of refuge or comfort? Or nothing at all?
Maybe the light was little from far, but up close was a fire
    That could warm to the bones.
"Over here! Over here!"
I thought about what I had which was practically nothing.
And looked back over there at what might just be something.
But without that first step out-
How would I know?

                    April 2, 2009

Move Mountain Move

I stood there boldly with my arms folded
And with the sternest, most electrifying, bone-chilling voice
I told that mountain to move…
"Move mountain move!"

…and it just laughed in my face.

So then I called my daddy,
But it was no longer in its place.

Jesus! Jesus! Jesus!

                        April 4, 2009

Rain

The trees love the rain,
    Birds take heavenly showers.
The waves get their strength,
    Rivers rush with power.
The grass becomes a drunk,
    Rain washes away earth's sorrow.
But the rain don't like me,
    Maybe there'll be joy tomorrow.

                    April 2, 2009

Chapter 4

Love

"He that loveth not knoweth not God; for God is love"

I John 4:8

"Love is patient and kind. Love is not jealous, it does not brag, and it is not proud. Love is not rude, is not selfish, and does not get upset with others. Love does not count up wrongs that have been done. Love takes no pleasure in evil but rejoices over the truth. Love patiently accepts all things. It always trusts, always hopes, and always endures. Love never ends..." (I Corinthians 13:4-8 NCV) God is love and love is all these things. When we learn to love, we should learn to love as God does, just as he loves us. Just as God loved Israel, which was his chosen people, he loves us just the same. He loved us so much that he gave his only son for us knowing that we were sinners. "But God commendeth his love toward us, in that, while we were yet sinners, Christ died for us." (Romans 5:8) God hates sin, so that says a lot for itself.

The expression of love can be explained many different ways. The world says love is a special date, a sexual relation, or the pride of a possession. Those things are temporary. Love never ends. The dictionary definition defines love as a noun, a feeling or pleasure. Love is an action, a verb, a to-do word. "For God so *loved*...he *gave* his only son," is an action. We do some of the things we do because we love. Saying you love someone is only a verbal expression of what you have to show. If you tell someone you love them and never show it, they don't feel like you love them at all. The action produces a feeling but the action must come first.

On the flip side of that is unconditional love. Meaning, no matter what, your feelings never change. That's the kind of love God has for us, "unconditional". No matter what we do, he still loves us. There is no action for unconditional love. You can't do anything to gain or lose it. For most parents, the love for a child is unconditional. We are God's children, which is why he loves us unconditionally. I couldn't even begin to explain how or why I love my children so much, I just do. Nothing they do could take my love from them. I can get angry or mad and even bitter with them, but I will always love them regardless.

Unconditional love comes from God; it is God's love and it lasts forever. If we could learn to love each other unconditionally, we have learned to love as God loves. "So these three things continue forever: faith, hope, and love. And the greatest of these is love." (I Corinthians 13:13 NCV)

The day my first child was born, I knew I would be able to love. I had struggled in the past showing love to anybody. All of my past relationships ended because I was never able to show enough affection or emotion. I was always told, "You don't care about anything". Harsh as it sounds, I don't think I ever did. However, when you look into the eyes of child, especially your child, everything changes. There are no negative feelings whatsoever, just pure love. Soon after that, I was married and my relationships with my family grew stronger. I became more conscious of how my actions affected other people. It wasn't until after I learned how to love that the Lord showed me how much he loves me.

I work the music at my church so I sit in the back behind everybody else. It is a somewhat secluded area with just the music and me. Music has the power to affect your thought process the moment you hear it. For instance, say you're driving down the road in a mellow and calm mood and then all of a sudden your favorite song plays on the radio. Now you're jumping up and down and singing your heart out to the open road. Well, a particular song was playing while I was in prayer and I caught myself praying the actual words to the song. I had tears streaming down my face but for some reason, something told me to get up, go get my daughter and just hug her and pray for her. My family was going through some tough financial times at that point in our lives.

Tears in my eyes, holding my daughter, and in deep prayer I heard the Lord say to me, "Look at your daughter. Do you see how much you love her?" I cried and cried. Like I said, we were going through a lot then and I just didn't know how we were going to make it. Then my pastor decided to come take my daughter from me and told me to just pray. As soon as he did I lifted my hands in prayer, but the Lord told me to put them down. Then he said, "Look at my hands, and he showed me the palms of my own hands. Do you see how much I love you?"

Follow Your Heart

Where do you find love?
Does love find you?
Which knows best, your heart or your mind?
The mind is trained, but the heart can be deceived.
It's always night and day between them.
Which one do you follow?
Can you go wrong letting your heart lead?

True happiness is in the heart.
Wills, cant's, and won't pierce like a dart.
Cupid's arrows find paths in the dark.
The heart speaks through your dreams, a canvas-less art.

As empty as a note-less staff, a quiet composition.
To play the music, to your heart you must listen.
Follow the beats, each strum in perfect position.
The mind plays tricks, the heart a continuous retention.

Like over and over or again and again.
The heart is the strength because the strength is within.
To have no beat is to end, for from the heart we begin.
From the beginning I will follow my heart to the end.

January 24, 2009

Why Did You Come Here?

Why did you come here? I wish you'd go back.
Go- before it's too late, but now it's too late for that.
Where were you before because it's not on the map?
You're going to love it here!
But I wish you'd go back…

Why did you come here? I can't help but wonder.
What could be so wrong with living above the thunder?
Did you come on purpose or a spiraling plunder?
Glad you were able to make it safely.
Though I can't help but wonder…

Why did you come here? I'm really confused.
Were you happy or sad when you heard the news?
Did you come here willingly or fight and refuse?
What took you so long!?
For real, I'm confused…

Why did you come here? I wish you'd have stayed.
What could be so intriguing you came to *this* place?
You just couldn't resist and had to show you face.
More beautiful than anything I've ever seen.
But I wish you'd have stayed…

December 4, 2008
…For Trinity & Adrianna…

Infatuation

Even if I never called, you were still on my mind.
Good times bad times you were still on my mind.
Tick-tock moving forward can't progress in rewind.
Wish I could press pause and you would still be mine.
Many a night we chilled bucket seats on recline.
Exchanged lust for the passion built over time.
Too young to recognize beauty's deeper than rind.
Maturity helps me learn how to pick up on love signs.

Years fade away but you were always there.
Whispering in my ears you were always there.
Taking everything for granted like I ain't care.
'Tho' I appreciated much, feelings are hard to share.
You understood every word with these bars I flare.
We were meant to be together from the very first glare.
First look was love, I knew because we both stared.
In my brain so much you're in my dreams and my nightmares…

Even if I never called I knew your voice was near.
Conversations all alone felt your voice was near.
Confused why we can't talk it wasn't always clear.
Argue and break-up then make-up like Sheer.
I still write to you log the month, day, and the year.
The letters never reach as pages in my notebook tear.
Life without you is just too hard to bear.
Tossing and turning when flashbacks appear.
I want you back there was no reason for you ever to leave.
We were perfect for each other why you have to leave.

Just you hopping in and out caused my heart to bleed.
I sell my soul for you down on a bended knee.
Don't act like we ain't have more love than beef.
Never ashamed mentioned your name all in these streets.
Matta' fact just being with you made a name for me.
Give me a second chance and I'll show you faithfully…

October 23, 2006

The Wise

So the old man asked,
"Who do you love?"
And he replied,
"I love myself… the only one who really cares about me."
…
"That's because you've never hated yourself," says the old man.

April 4, 2009

Dear Brother

Dear Brother,
Tho' I've never seen your face, you are dear to me
You've stood beside me all along and stayed near to me
A brother's love is harsh you've kept it real with me
And helped me to see life through the true reality

Dear Brother,
You are wise well beyond your years
In your youth excelled among your peers
Tho' I've never seen you shed one tear
You've had your share of pain and fear

Dear Brother,
You bring our family great honor
You are the crown of a million fathers
Clay craftily molded by the divine potter
The dust does not deserve your sons or daughters

Dear Brother,
One day we will see each other again
Because I am you if you are within
Stronger than all of earth's men
Keep me by your side until we meet again

April 5, 2009

Chapter 5

Forgiveness

*"For if ye forgive men their trespasses,
your heavenly Father will also forgive you:
but if ye forgive not men their trespasses,
neither will your Father forgive your trespasses."*

Matthew 6:14-15

"If you, LORD, kept a record of sins, Lord, who could stand? But with you there is forgiveness, so that we can, with reverence, serve you." (Psalm 130:3-4 NIV) The Lord would rather not punish but forgive. In our sins, we constantly stir up the wrath of God, but his love and mercy toward us are greater than his anger. "But he, being full of compassion, forgave their iniquity, and destroyed them not: yea, many a time turned he his anger away, and did not stir up all his wrath." (Psalm 78:38) God gives us plenty of chances to change our ways. How can we expect to be forgiven if we never change? He tugs at us daily on one side while the world pulls at the other. Even if we turn our back to him and walk the other way, he will happily accept us back and all of heaven will rejoice. The more he forgives, the more we learn to love him back; but if he only forgave us a few times and never again, we would be less likely to want to return to God. "…but to whom little is forgiven, the same loveth little." (Luke 7:47)

Also, how can you expect to be forgiven if you don't forgive others? "And be ye kind one to another, tenderhearted, forgiving one another, even as God for Christ sake hath forgiven you." (Ephesians 4:32) I know this contradicts the ways of the world that teach you to get revenge, accept no disrespect, and love only those who show love to you. This is a prime example of why the ways of the world and the ways of God cannot be mixed. Think of yourself and all the things you've done and been through. If God never gave you a second chance or never forgave you then follow the world, but if he did, why do you keep going back to the ones that didn't. "…Repent, and turn yourselves from all your transgressions; so iniquity shall not be your ruin. Cast away from you all your transgressions, whereby ye have transgressed; and make you a new heart and a new spirit: for why will ye die, O house of Israel? For I have no pleasure in the death of him that dieth, saith the Lord GOD: wherefore turn yourselves, and live ye." (Ezekiel 18:30-32)

When I look back at all the things I've done and been through; and I think back on all the things I've tried to accomplish ending up back on square one every time, I use to wonder, what in the world am I doing wrong? Now when I look back again, and this time thinking if God was in it, I realize God must have been frustrated with me. I was hardheaded, trying to do things my own way. He just kept shaking me up and returning me to that old square one to try it again, I mean every time. I thought I had it when I was in school, wrong! I thought I was good when I went into the military, wrong! I thought this was it for sure doing music, wrong again! Not one time did I even ask God, "is this where you want me", or "what do you want me to do". He kindly just led me back toward him because he knew what was in my heart and he knew what might have been waiting for me on the other side: pride wanted to take away my heart, lust tried to pollute my brain, and death was in my bed waiting for me to lie down. God saw fit for me to live and gave me another chance to turn to him once more. And when I did, when I finally did, he opened up, poured out his Word on me, and blessed me more than I could ever imagine. I realized how much he had forgiven me of and I loved him even more.

G.R.I.T.S.

Father up above is there room for me?
Was I born with more sins than the man standing next to me?
Pray for me, or does your only son mean one?
Why do you seem harder to reach for people in the slums?
The ghettos filled with drugs there's no escape from guns.
We never see your light shine the darkness don't run.
Waiting for the day you come through,
Remember my name, can't hear you say "I never knew you".

    Gracefully, I bow down to the Lord above
    Right or wrong in the decisions I make I am still his son
    Insecurities and difficulties along the way
    Trials and tribulations he'd never lead me astray
    Still I live through his grace to see another day…

    God, dear Lord, please forgive me for my sins past and future
    Restore my broken pieces so that I may be whole and pure
    I may seem incomplete to the rest of the world I face
    Time passes and each second is one closer to your gates
    Still I live through your grace to see another day…

    Greed, anger, and hate I've learned to dismiss Lord
    Renew me daily Lord, so that I may,
    Inhabit the blessings you have for me Lord
    Trust in me not to deceive my fellow man for gain
    So that I may live through your grace to see another day…

    Guide me Lord through the path of righteousness
    Remember me Lord as I pray for your forgiveness
    I pray that you also keep your hand over my family
    Those blood and those who loved me as family
    So that we may live through your grace to see another day…

Give thanks to you dear Lord for all things
Regardless big or small because you are the provider of all
Inside and out Lord, you alone know my true heart and soul
Teach me to use this temple for your will
So that I may live through your grace to see another day…

Father up above is there room for me?
Was I born with more sins than the man standing next to me?
Pray for me, or does your only son mean one?
Why do you seem harder to reach for people in the slums?
The ghettos filled with drugs there's no escape from guns.
We never see your light shine the darkness don't run.
Waiting for the day you come through,
Remember my name, can't hear you say "I never knew you".

September 7, 2006

Spiritual Simplicity

I don't know why I ask questions but I do.
Sometimes I hear a voice and wonder Lord is it you
Lord you know I don't have any trouble doing Your will,
I will,
    What you ask of me.
Even if I did, it's because I'm only human.
If I could see it through my Father's eyes,
    Your will would be done.

Please forgive my mind for its ignorance.
My heart apologizes for its selective deafness.
My eyes are sorry...
    They forget where to look.
My feet used to walk with you...
    They've gotten lost.

At one point these hands could feel your pain...
    They've gone numb.
Out of my mouth was your Word...
    Still searching for restoration,
My soul is a reflection of your work... though I wonder,
    "Did I get fired?"

Saturate my mind in your conscious Word.
Open the ears of my heart so your voice can be heard.
Give me tunnel vision; I'll look straight to you always.
Lead my feet, so sore from walking in the wrong direction,
    Back to you.

Provide the nerves in my hands feeling
    Enough to reach out and touch you.
Restore your Word in my tongue so people know
    You speak thru me.
I don't want to quit Lord.
Continue your work in me.
Now and forever

                      April 5, 2009

Release Me

Renew in me a clean spirit, Oh Lord
For I have fallen into an ungodly ward
A prison, no doubt,
    Evil patrols the gates
No windows and no doors
    Keep me from seeing your face
But you are in my heart
    A place their bonds are powerless
Look down on your servant with mercy and forgiveness
Confess I unto you, praying release me
    Release me
'Lest I dash my feet,' trouble I trample beneath me

Renew in me a clean spirit, Oh Lord
For all my strength was in your Word
A refuge, no doubt,
    With holiness inside the gates
On the countryside in a valley
    For everyone to escape
But you are in my heart
    A place their bonds are powerless
Look down on your servant with mercy and forgiveness
Address I unto you, praying release me
    Release me
Send me your Spirit, trouble I trample beneath me

                May 9, 2009

Forgive Me

My hope for death could never be more sincere
Only fear keeps me from wanting to go near

I have sinned Father,
    Forgive me!

Will even the dust remember my name?
Will even my spirit remember everything
    It worked so hard to gain?

I can only be sure in the thought that God knows
I can plant the seed but only God makes it grow

I have sinned Father,
    Forgive me!

Did it all go according to plan?
Did you know that one day
    I would understand?

I strive for holiness and perfection in the sight of the most high
I would hope for death but I don't want to be judged
    guilty when I die

I have sinned Father,
    Forgive me!

                    May 13, 2009

The Rope

Draw back your bow, oh Lord.
    It has been ready for a long time
        Piercing the wicked with fatal precision.

Use me…
Give me the power to change and save.
    You can start with me.

My heart cries for the blood of my people
    Led into temptation and death.
If you can show me, and I can learn,
    Can they not learn also?
The rope of the unrighteous tugs at us daily,
    Tightening the grip around our necks.

Give me the sword to cut it…
Show me how to use it…

If not for just one?
    Just one Lord!
If not for just one?

Use me…
And I will cut mine last!

                    May 15, 2009

Chapter 6

Change

"If my people, which are called by my name, shall humble themselves, and pray, and seek my face, and turn from their wicked ways; then I will hear from heaven, and will forgive their sin, and will heal their land."

II Chronicles 7:14

"...If any man will come after me, let him deny himself, and take up his cross daily, and follow me." (Luke 9:23) Everyone comes to a crossroad in their life where they must make a life-changing decision. Should you go left or should you go right? Usually there is no turning back from either decision. But it's not the decision that makes a difference in your life; it's what you do after you make the decision that determines whether the choice you made was a good one. Change is a process and does not occur overnight. Follow through with your decisions and you will see the process of change in your life. God wants us to change but he himself does not change because God does not sin. "For I am the Lord, I change not..." (Malachi 3:6)

Repentance is a sign of a changed heart. The Lord wants us all to repent for our sins, which is asking for forgiveness and desiring in your heart a willingness to change your ways. He patiently waits for us to repent and turn to him. "...joy shall be in heaven over one sinner that repenteth..." (Luke 15:7) "...except ye repent, ye shall all likewise perish." (Luke 13:3) God does not want us to die and be judged guilty of sin, He gives us opportunity after opportunity to change our ways we just have to be willing to do so. "For godly sorrow worketh repentance to salvation not to be repented of: but the sorrow of the world worketh death." (II Corinthians 7:10)

After you ask God to forgive you and work to change your ways, then you must be baptized. Baptism is a sign of your agreement with God that you will diligently try to obey him and turn from a sinful life. It is symbolic for the death of the flesh, which is sin, and the birth of the Spirit, which is the Lord, in you. Once you've made your agreement with the Lord you allow him to work in you by opening up your heart to his word. "...Repent, and be baptized every one of you in the name of Jesus Christ for the remission of sins, and ye shall receive the gift of the Holy Ghost." (Acts 2:38)

"He that believeth and is baptized shall be saved..." (Mark 16:16) The Lord came to me one day while I was taking a shower and said to me, "You have to genuinely believe that I am, I died, and have risen." As the water went down my face, I started to imagine pictures of death and being raised up from the dead. I couldn't tell you what the pictures looked like, but all I can remember is the image of me being raised up out of the water. I thought to myself, if I believe with my whole heart that the Lord lives, I should be baptized. I was baptized once already when I was young, but I didn't fully understand the meaning then. God wanted me to show my agreement with him for him to work in my life. In other words, all he needed was for me to sign the contract stating, "I will let you in my heart Lord".

  Five of us were baptized in a lake out in the public for all to see. I struggled trying not to think of what people may have thought or if they were laughing or anything of that sort. All I wanted was to show God this is who I am, and I no longer want to live the way I was before, and I open up my heart to you. I was told as soon as we began the baptisms everyone at the lake became quiet and watched, almost as if showing respect for the work of God. Even people out on their boats came in to see. I've never felt anything more peaceful as I did when I entered the water. Nobody said a word but everyone watched.

Sometimes

Sometimes,
We will lose a piece of ourselves and find our whole
Or lose our whole trying to find that one piece.

Sometimes,
We will put all we have into nothing
And put nothing into what we already have.

Sometimes,
We will pray for a change today and tomorrow do the same thing
Or pray for a change tomorrow and today do nothing.

Sometimes,
We will search for something old and find something new
Or search for something new and find something old.

Sometimes,
When others hope for life just going through the day
We will go through life and hope for better days.

Sometimes,
We will want more than what we can have
But have more than what we could ever want.

Sometimes,
We wish we had more sometimes!

December 15, 2007

The Church

The people are the *BODY* of the church.
Lord be our bodies.
Your Spirit is the *VOICE* of the church.
Lord speak through us.
Your Word is the *FOOD* of the church.
Lord fill us 'til we want no more.
Praise is the *FIRE* of the church.
Lord burn everlasting.
Understanding is the *STRENGTH* of the church.
Lord be our rock.
Tears are the *LIFE* of the church.
Lord let your blood be in us.
Testimony is the *RESULT* of the church.
Lord make us new…again.

February 22, 2009

The Caterpillar

Remind me of the caterpillar once again.
He crawled and crawled from leaf to stem.
Time moved fast, but he passed by slow.
Did he know about the day that he would grow?
The more he ate the slower he got.
He just had to eat and he ate a lot.
It was his nature so simple and plain.
Did he know about the day that he would change?
Gaining strength, even more with each bite.
Wished he was like the ant, but this was his life.
Until one day he could barely move, he had to rest.
Did he know about the day that he would be blessed?
He slept and slept and slept for a very long time.
His body kept changing until he could one day fly.
He awoke from his sleep when he could sleep no more.
Did he know about the day that he would once soar?

Could I be like the caterpillar, my patience you test?
I'll eat just as much knowledge. You give and I get.
Time moves fast and I learn, it seems, slow.
Did you know about the day that I would grow?
Feed me your Word and I'll keep it within.
Teach me to love as you say you did.
Not like before; too much hurt too much pain.
Did you know about the day that I would change?
I'm your beacon of light waiting to shine bright.
But not like the others who fade in the night.
Faith is my patience, my patience you test.
Did you know about the day that I would be blessed?
On you I meditate and pray for success.
Success first in spirit and then life nonetheless.
Use me and use me until your will is no more
Did you know about the day that I would once soar?

February 10, 2009
Dedicated to Daisy Adella "Aiken" Campbell

Stable Mind

A stable mind is an able mind
    Willing and kind
Finds the simple things in life that shines
Like the smile on the face of a newborn
    So innocent
Good times, those never die, recycling…
    Remembering…

                              December 28, 2006

Birth'd in the Grave

You've given birth to me in the grave.
    I emerged changed and saved.

Water is life,
    But I was born and died ablaze.

Refreshing is the touch
Of the 'cool hand' on my face.

Cover me, and then free me,
    Deliverance is in this place.

                          June 4, 2009

Chapter 7

Commitment

*"Trust in the Lord with all thine heart;
and lean not unto thine own understanding.
In all thy ways acknowledge him, and
he shall direct thy paths."*

Proverbs 3:5-6

"...The Lord is with you, while ye be with him; and if ye seek him, he will be found of you; but if you forsake him, he will forsake you." (II Chronicles 15:2) "For the eyes of the Lord run to and fro throughout the whole earth, to shew himself strong in the behalf of them whose heart is perfect toward him..." (II Chronicles 16:9) God is looking for loyal souls that follow him with their whole heart. Loyalty proves your commitment and builds trust. If you can't trust God, how can you expect him to trust in you to do his will and receive your reward? Whatever your heart trusts in is whom it will serve and follow. If you trust in God, you will follow the Word, but if you trust in the world, you will follow the world.

Trusting is also an essential part of belief. Where there is no trust there is no truth, where there is no truth there is no belief, and where there is no belief there is no commitment. Trust that God can do; believe he will do; and he will do what you ask. "Ask, and it shall be given you; seek, and ye shall find; knock, and it shall be opened unto you: for every one that asketh receiveth; and he that seeketh findeth; and to him that knocketh it shall be opened." (Matthew 7:7-8)

Relationships are built on trust. God wants to build a relationship with each and every one of us. How can we say that we love God if we follow everything the world does? Luckily, he loves us unconditionally or else we would all have a hard time gaining God's mercy and grace. He waits until the Day of Judgment to cut off those whom he's never had a relationship. "...I never knew you: depart from me, ye that work iniquity." (Matthew 7:23) But, if we are with the Lord, he will strengthen us here on earth to do his will and provide everything we need. "...as long as he sought the LORD, God made him to prosper." (II Chronicles 26:5) Then when he judges us, he will know us by name.

One time the Lord came to me and asked me, "If you can't commit to anything, how will you commit to me?" I didn't know the answer. I thought back on all the things I've done or tried to do in my life. Pretty much everything I ever wanted to accomplish, I never did. All the small things I finished, but I ended up quitting everything that took hard work and long-term dedication.

Short-term hard work I could handle, but continuous struggle to achieve, I needed help. And as far as relationships, forget it, I never committed to any of them. The relationship I was in at the time the Lord asked me that question, was the longest I had ever been in. I tried to leave that one too but the significant other wasn't having that. We were actually talking marriage, children and a home. All long term commitments.

The day the Lord asked me, "how will you commit to me," made me think of all the things I could try to commit to. That way I could show myself worthy of a faithful commitment. After a lot of careful consideration, I decided marriage would be best. I loved the woman I was with and she loved me and we had already been through enough together, so why not? I prayed about it and God gave me an answer. The only thing that was in the way was the money for the ring so I could propose. I knew she would say "yes" already because she had been talking about it since forever, but a proposal is essential.

I didn't want to just go up to her and say, "Hey, marry me!" and walk away. One day I was going through some old cards and I found one from the year before that was for my birthday. It was from my now mother-in-law. The card read, "Thanks for making our daughter happy!" and it still had the money in it she had given me, enough for the ring.

Generation

If I quit now, then who is left to teach you?
If I give up now, then who is left to reach you?
I'll show you the stars and everything that lies beneath you.
Life is the achievement if you can see it in complete view.

Be the first to break the chain;
Only leaders can bring a change.
I'll mold your internal frame;
Spiritual mind is a golden gain.
Be the dewdrops and the rain;
Ambitious drives with no restrain.
Holding on is to maintain;
Be the pupil aboard the train.

If I quit now, then who is left to teach you?
If I give up now, then who is left to reach you?
I'll show you the stars and everything that lies beneath you.
Life is the achievement if you can see it in complete view.

April 15, 2009

My Shoes

My shoes are worn, the road is dirty
Working all night and still wake up early

No sleep, I'm using every minute of the light
Trying to be constructive every second of my life

Using what was given and making the best of what I've got
No time to waste, there are still conflicts in the plot

Reach the resolution when the Father calls me home
Until then, there are things to do and places to roam

October 27, 2005

Broken Pieces

Tried by fire produces quite a sting,
    But to come out clean
    Now that is the purest thing.

Gather up the broken pieces
    And mold them back together;
The potter's hand is steady
    Flawless design with each endeavor.

                      May 24, 2009

Blessed

Blessed be the name of the Lord:
    Whose might knows no limits,
    Whose hands can reach beyond
        The depths of the sea and the stars in the sky,
    Whose wisdom reigns supreme
        Searching the hearts of man
        Calling out to those who diligently seek him.

May the Lord be praised forever among all man.
    And may his mercy be upon us always,
    Lest we be found evil in the sight of the Lord.

Amen.

                      May 25, 2009

Silence

The power of silence

Silence can be felt…
Silence can be felt…

When you move I do not speak…
When you move I do not speak…

On my tongue,
Stretch forth the burning rod
"Be still and know that I am God"

Are the praises of the angels in heaven not enough
    That you still desire my praise
Shouting hallelujah in the highest voice eternally
    But you'd rather number my days
Spare not the rod and spoil the child
    Your faithful servant follows your ways
Are the praises of the angels in heaven not enough
    That you still desire my praise

The power of silence
    Silence can be felt…

                June 13, 2009

Chapter 8

Sacrifice

"And he said to them all, If any man will come after me, let him deny himself, and take up his cross daily, and follow me."

Luke 9:23

"For a just man falleth seven times and riseth up again: but the wicked shall fall into mischief."(Proverbs 24:16) When you have nothing to lose and everything to gain, where do you turn for restoration? Do you go back to the things that let you down once already, or do you seek out that which has the promise of life more abundantly? God does not give us more than he knows we can handle. Any trouble we go through is to strengthen us for a greater trouble ahead in life and for us to turn to God, who will prove himself worthy of bringing us out. You'll never know that he can bring you through it if he doesn't allow you to go into it. If you don't turn to God in your time of trouble, where does your help come from? If you do succeed in coming out of it, will you be strong enough to go through it again or something even greater? Did you learn from it or do just enough to make it through?

Suffering is not the same as sacrifice, but sometimes sacrifice takes you through a bit of suffering. Suffering lets you know that all sacrifices are not easy. If the poor and suffering are no longer poor and suffering, will they remember from whence they came? Most will not want to look back on their times of trouble. We should not look back on the evil we did to devise a better evil plan, but we should look back to learn from our mistakes. If a child never realizes their mistakes, how will they ever know not to do wrong? Sometimes punishment is necessary for learning. You can tell a child something a hundred times and it have no effect; but you give them an example, then they will learn. As God's children, the teachings are no different. Times of trouble and distress are the times when we should be learning the most. "...What? Shall we receive good at the hand of God, and shall we not receive evil? ..." (Job 2:10) If you call on God in your time of trouble, lesson learned. "My son, despise not the chastening of the LORD; neither be weary of his correction: For whom the Lord loveth he correcteth; even as a father the son in whom he delighteth." (Proverbs 3:11-12)

It's amazing how much a child can teach you about yourself without saying a word. Everything you are, you know, what you grew up on is put into that child, and whatever you put in will eventually come out. We basically sacrifice everything we are to put ourselves into our children, either to prepare them for the life we've lived, or train them for the life we wanted to live, or both. A child adheres to the words of a parent, teacher, mentor, or coach. Children of God are to be the same way.

I asked the Lord one night, "Lord, what made me stop and just turn to you no looking back? How did I even start writing this book?" It was a restless night and I had been visiting the past in my mind, realizing my mistakes. I was pretty selfish back then, but I was young and most young people are. The world teaches us to reach our goals and be somebody, so my life and my accomplishments were top of the list to me. The words of my parents, especially the Word of God, fell on deaf ears at those times.

I started feeling like Israel and I had gotten upset with my past. Defending myself, I told the Lord, "Well, Jesus already knew the Word coming into the world so it was easier to resist the temptations of a man." Thinking selfishly again, I tried to give an excuse for my sins. And he responded so calmly saying, "Yes, he did, and he still decided that it was better to obey and do the will of God than give into the flesh." Jesus sacrificed himself so the will of God would be done. He knew the Word and decided the cause was worth more than self. Jesus already knew the sacrifice for salvation was his life.

If I Could Have A Dime

If I could have a dime for every time I felt underrated
Like a puppet on display with bright lights and big stages.

Chains with open cages and the world to roam
But the only way to find peace is to sleep with the bones.

    Could I buy my way out? ...

What's the legal tender in heaven?
One shot will stop your future and put an end to your presence.

The present is a gift, longevity…the essence.
Life is worth much more than diamonds in a necklace.

So to what is the price on my barcode connected,
If my soul is uplifted and my body is rejected?

Innocence neglected, we were all born defective
Guilty with no charge since a baby so precious.

But what about all the times that I was plainly disrespected
Over-worked and under-paid, overlooked or drug tested?

Judged by a message to TV image perfections.
Religious made standards by man-made reflections.

What would be the point in ballin' if all the money's for weapons?
Sell your soul to the devil, but can't sell it to get to heaven.

September 22, 2008

Fortunate

I'm fortunate to not have a fortune
I'm fortunate to struggle everyday and let God be my portion
I'm fortunate to still have a prayer
I'm fortunate to know that even if I didn't He'd still be there
I'm fortunate for eyes that can see
I'm fortunate for ears that can hear and a mouth that can speak
    Legs that can run and feet when I need to take a stand
I'm fortunate to be in God's plan.

                  September 11, 2008

Old Soul

Lord,
    Why'd you give me this old soul?

Bones about as brittle as a chewed up #2 pencil
Seem like free hand but I feel like a stencil
Ol' sore and achy back and tiresome feet
I'd run like the wind if you'd stop aging me
    Not yet though!

Lord,
    I guess I'll keep this old soul?

                      April 16, 2009

Jericho

Unchain these shackles
Break down these walls

Oh Jericho, when will you fall?

I've been down for so long
Walked seven times and still goin'

Oh Jericho, when will you fall?

I think it's time to come down
I think it's time to come down

Oh Jericho, when will you fall?

Blow the trumpets…

                                        April 17, 2009

That's What I Call Pain

Pull the knife out of your back
    It won't hurt if you do it fast
But you'll bleed a whole lot more
    And you might not last

Pull the stake out of your heart
    It won't hurt if you do it fast
But you'll be left with a hole
    To remember the past

Pull the nails out of your hands
    It won't hurt if you do it fast
But you'll suffer with the pain
    Of all the sins you have to bear

Pull the thorns out of your head
    It won't hurt if you do it fast
But you'll be left with the thought
    Of all the ones who didn't care

April 28, 2009

Chapter 9

Obedience

"Thy word have I hid in mine heart, that I might not sin against thee."

Psalm 119:11

"…Hath the LORD as great delight in burnt offerings and sacrifices, as in obeying the voice of the Lord? Behold, to obey is better than sacrifice, and to hearken than the fat of rams." (I Samuel 15:22) "Blessed are they that keep his testimonies, and seek him with the whole heart." (Psalm 119:2) God desires our hearts. If you can open your heart to him, he will open up his heart to you. He can bless us far more than we could ever bless him. It is not easy obeying God's word when you try to hold on to the things of the world and obey him.. God's agenda is not the same as the world's. "No man can serve two masters: for either he will hate the one, and love the other; or else he will hold on to the one, and despise the other. Ye cannot serve God and mammon." (Matthew 6:24) The world cannot understand God's purpose. The Lord has good reason for us to obey him, not just so we can be good citizens, but for the salvation of our souls.

The only ones who fully understand sin and its consequences are God, the devil, and the dead. God wants us to be with him; he loves us. The devil is just looking for power. We must obey every word of the voice of the Lord in order to come to him. "…It is written; Man shall not live by bread alone, but by every word that proceedeth out of the mouth of God'." (Matthew 4:4) He leads us by his voice. It is a peaceful voice like a mother's voice calling out to her children. The voice of the world is loud and alluring, deceiving you into a life full of sin. "For the wages of sin is death; but the gift of God is eternal life through Jesus Christ our Lord." (Romans 6:23)

I was in a church service of five people and the Lord spoke to me, "Be the guide I made you to be; the time is now!" It was something I had been praying about for a while. "Lord what do you want me to do, which way do you want me to go," I'd asked the Lord night and day, trying to figure out my purpose on this earth. Everything else I've tried to do just didn't work out as I planned and I kept coming back to square one. This time I decided I'd wait on the Lord to give me an answer because I've come too close to too many near death encounters trying to do things my own way. That church service had just enough people in it for the Lord to come directly to each one of us and speak. Then he spoke to the congregation as a whole. The purpose God has for you is not only for you, but he is using you to reach somebody else. Two witnesses can reach twice as many people than one person can.

Silent Weapon

My tongue is like a two-edged sword. I'll slice you
    And then slice you again.
        Ya dig!
Better yet,
It's got the sting of a dragon and the force of the ocean.
    There is no stopping me!
Beware of what you speak because my tongue spits back.
Instinctively I war words, and knight verbs, and form armies
    And navies with nouns and syllables.
        Dig that!
Lyrically I'm unbound, untamed…
Too wild a beast for the zoo,
    And too subtle and conniving for the jungle.
Rumble, humble as a mumble, a ninja with language;
Words come off of my tongue as rolling thunder.
Fierce and raw,
Yet can be as gentle as a drizzle.
Come for comfort or affliction; pierce like a Gensu blade.
I'll cut your heart in the worst way.
My tongue…
Oh my tongue can break ya pride tough guy,
    Build your character, teach wisdom and correction,
    Stay on your mind even after the fact, a life lesson,
    Give you that stepping stone, or cut your progression.
Stop right there!
Do Not Advance!
I can command you or command millions.
I can cause oppressed people to think,
    Leave their homes, and become pilgrims.
Yo soy malo y bueno cual quiera quiero ser.
Muerta y vida esta en el poder de la lengua:
y los quien les gusta comerán de la fruta.

Death and life are in the power of the tongue:
and they that love it shall eat the fruit thereof.

                February 22, 2009

Flaws

Man has flaws,
    God does not!
Follow in the ways of the lost,
    Burning hot!
Getting warm like the burner lift the,
    Boiling pot!
Keep standing in the flames until ya,
    Scorch ya socks!
If you thinking you can take it you a,
    Melting rock!
God's a solid foundation sin,
    Stumbles and drops!
False sense of elevation until you,
    Plummet and flop!
Even sitting on the peak you can,
    Fall off the top!!!

                December 28, 2006

Exodus

I know he's calling my name
    I can hear him just plain
I'm asking send for me Father
    He says you have to maintain
You got to do all the things
    I put you on earth to do
After you done all you can do
Then son you got to stay true

So I plan my escape
    For when I'm leaving this place
Just give me the words and the path
    And all the routes I can take
Headed straight for the promise land
    Where my soul can feel safe
On this earth I don't feel anything
    But more pain and disgrace

Pushing on day to day
    Lord just lead on the way
If I put my heart in it
    How could I go astray
Pressures down here are tough
    Nobody is thinking of you
But I'm a do all I can do
    Looking to you staying true

                    May 7, 2009

Ignorance

One day a woman was praying to the Lord
    For she was going through some troubling times.
She prayed and prayed even read her Word
    Figured she'd just have to wait in line.

Oh this woman was full of sorrow, built up for many years.
    But what you've been through is not important,
    Sometimes it's what you've learned.
Never had a day of dry eyes, seem all she got was tears.
    She prayed and prayed even read her Word
    Figured she'd just have to wait her turn.

A heavy heart that asks, the Lord just can't ignore.
    He heard her all along and remembered her every cry.
Lord says it's time now and sent and angel to her door
    At three o' clock in the morning on a cold, stormy night.

She was sleeping peacefully when she heard the knocks.
    Got up and looked outside and seen a man standing there.
She shooed him off and sent him home for it was three o' clock.
    He cried out, "I need your help its cold and wet out here!"

"I have no home, no clothes, no food I need a place to rest.
    I won't stay long soon I'll be gone and continue on my way."
For three days straight he asked of her, she cancelled all request.
    Still all the while full of sadness, on her knees she'd pray.

One more time the angel knocked, this time he called her name.
    You were so full of sadness of what you ask you could not give.
The Lord has heard your prayers and sent me to your place.
    You were so full of sorrow of what you ask you could not give.

I came for peace and comfort, refuge, warmth, and love.
    You were so full of sadness, what you ask you could not give.
How can you ask for the same from the Lord up above?
    You were so full of sorrow, what you ask you could not give.

April 7, 2009

Humbled

The eagle's home is built
    Closest to heaven.
But its food is on the ground
    And in the sea.

                        May 26, 2009

Chapter 10

Works

"Be confident of this very thing, that he which hath begun a good work in you will perform it until the day of Jesus Christ."

Philippians 1:6

Everything we are able to do Christ put in us as gifts; we make up a perfect Christ when we use our gifts together. The Spirit of the Lord uses people in different ways to make unbelievers believe. Those that do believe, through the will of God, use the gifts he gave to further their understanding of his will. "Now there are diversities of gifts, but the same Spirit. And there are differences of administration, but the same Lord. And there are diversities of operations but it is the same God which worketh all in all." (I Corinthians 12:4-6) When you bring your gifts together, through the divine will and order of the Lord, they make up a church. The church is the body of Christ. No one member is more important or less important than the other. "But now are they many members, yet but one body." (I Corinthians 12:20) Just like a human body, every member must play their part. "For the Son of Man shall come in the glory of his Father with his angels; and then he shall reward every man according to his works." (Matthew 16:27)

It is said that when a person loses one sense, such as sight, the other senses become stronger; or when one part of the body suffers the whole body suffers. The same goes for the body of Christ, the body of the church. The body struggles to operate when one member is missing or inoperable. It would be difficult to use your hands if you were missing your thumbs. In a church, it would be hard to conduct praise and worship with no songs and no music. The Spirit of the Lord moves as your spirit moves. Whether you sing, speak, or greet people as they walk in the door, the Lord can move through you just to reach one person, one non-believer. But you must make yourself operable, a functioning member in the body of Christ, in order for your gifts, or your works, to be of any use in the Kingdom of God. He gave you the gift to do the work. "For as the body without the spirit is dead, so faith without works is dead also." (James2:26)

The Lord gave me this one Sunday afternoon: "The creator makes the work; how then is the work to say to the creator, I am what I am? The creator owns the work; how then is the work to say to the creator, I do what I want?" I thought on how true that is. How can we go through life planning our own lives, when we were already created to be a part of God's plan? He taught me that in January. It wasn't until June of the same year that I read a similar passage in Isaiah. You were created with a purpose. We are the works of God. We were made according to his design and in his own image as the Bible says in Genesis 1:26. Who are we to tell him who we are and what we will do with our lives?

Israel Me

My fathers were in bondage over 400 years
They cried to the Lord and he dried up their tears
My mothers were in bondage over 400 years
They cried to the Lord and we are still here

Israel cried and the Lord delivered
Israel turned and the Lord forgiveth

Where is the Lord?
    I know that he's near
Me be like Israel is that what you fear?
God does not fear, my heart he can see
Looked right into it, is Israel me?
Lord I can change, would you save one?
Then he replied, "I sent you my son."

My fathers were in bondage over 400 years
They cried to the Lord and he dried up their tears
My mothers were in bondage over 400 years
They cried to the Lord and we are still here

Israel cried and the Lord delivered
Israel turned and the Lord forgiveth
Where is the Lord?
    My children not safe
Me be like Israel I'm leaving this place

Laws may have changed but the concept is "free'
I will not serve your gods, is Israel me?
Lord we need Moses to help us get through
Then he replied, "I already sent you!"

April 23, 2009

Regard

The notes of my Madrigal
Are duty sincere
Cherish the ones you have
Take it from me you will be glad

When they are gone
You soon will long

It's a calamity
To have something grabbed from thee
That you thought would
Never leave

Retrieve the reason
Before the end of the season
When the sun come up
Don't count your luck

Cede the need
To feel the need to lead

Flattery is not sound you see,
Used it will cost a fee

Banish the lisp talk
And find a new walk

Lose the fleck you
And you will be
Seen flamboyantly

Find the hidden stile of life
And regain your sight
Soon to be banished
By those infuriated

Inherit the sense of comfort
That has now been delivered

Written By: Tiffany Maybank

Tap, Tap, Tap!

Tap, Tap, Tap! ... Tap, Tap, Tap! ...
I hear the rain on my window pane.
Tap, Tap, Tap! ... Tap, Tap, Tap! ...
I was too tired I just rolled over again.
Tap, Tap, Tap! ... Tap, Tap, Tap! ...
It was almost melodic, meditative as it repeats.
Tap, Tap, Tap! ... Tap, Tap, Tap! ...
I didn't budge; I was too deep in my sleep.

Wake up! Wake up son, can you hear me?
I'm calling out to you, come near me.
It's time now. I heard you when you called.
I thought you said you would wait up for my response.
Tap, Tap, Tap! ... Tap, Tap, Tap! ...
My timing is perfect. Now our work can be done.
I came but you weren't ready, wake up before I'm gone.

Can you hear me in your dreams?
Now I wait for you it seems.
You asked and now I am here.
I'm calling out to you…come near.

Tap, Tap, Tap! ... Tap, Tap, Tap! ...
I hear the rain on my windowpane.
Tap, Tap, Tap! ... Tap, Tap, Tap! ...
I was too tired I just rolled over again.
Tap, Tap, Tap! ... Tap, Tap, Tap! ...
It was almost melodic, meditative as it repeats.
Tap, Tap, Tap! ... Tap, Tap, Tap! ...
I didn't budge; I was too deep in my sleep.

Lord where are you? I called but you didn't come.
Why did you leave me hanging have you no compassion for your son?
You called me and I came, I know I heard you say my name.
I looked but couldn't find you; is this some guessing game?
Tap, Tap, Tap! … Tap, Tap, Tap! …
If I ask I should receive and if I knock you would open.
I didn't know it'd take this long and you would leave me here hoping.
I'm not trying to rush you, but I'm getting sleepy you see.
I know you're very busy so I'll wait until you get to me.

Tap, Tap, Tap! … Tap, Tap, Tap! …
I hear the rain on my window pane.
Tap, Tap, Tap! … Tap, Tap, Tap! …
I was too tired I just rolled over again.
Tap, Tap, Tap! … Tap, Tap, Tap! …
It was almost melodic, meditative as it repeats.
Tap, Tap, Tap! … Tap, Tap, Tap! …
I didn't budge; I was too deep in my sleep.

March 16, 2009

The Ways of Man

The ways of man…
    Define a law and then break it
    Enforce a punishment and then change it
    Pass judgment and then rename it
    Take credit for a creation and then proclaim it
    Gain knowledge and then frame it
    Teach the ways of another man and then grade it
    Destroy the place of kings and then replace it

                March 1, 2009

Job Fair

I would rather practice being a
 Janitor on earth…

 And clean up in heaven…

Than be a CEO
 And own a company in hell.

May 17, 2009

Chapter II

Into The Light

*"...I am the light of the world:
he that followeth me shall not walk in darkness,
but shall have the light of life."*

John 8:12

"This then is the message which we have heard of him, and declare unto you, that God is light, and in him is no darkness at all. If we say that we have fellowship with him, and walk in darkness, we lie, and do not the truth: But if we walk in the light, as he is in the light, we have fellowship one with another and the blood of Jesus Christ his Son cleanses us from all sin." (I John 1:5-7) "And this is the condemnation, that light is come into the world, and men loved darkness rather than light, because their deeds were evil. For every one that doeth evil hateth the light neither cometh to the light, lest his deeds should be reproved. But he that doeth truth cometh to the light, that his deeds may be made manifest, that they are wrought in God." (John 3:19-21)

Have you ever heard the expression, "walk away from the light"? When someone loses consciousness, sometimes they say they saw a light coming toward them. To go towards the light means you're dead and to walk away means you're alive. Spiritually it's the opposite; we are to walk toward the light. To walk away from the light means you're dead spiritually and to walk toward the light means you're alive spiritually. Sin buries you in darkness, but God is the light and the way out of sin. Those who do wrong usually try to hide what they have done. Those who have done nothing wrong don't have anything to hide. If your judgment was today would you run and hide or could you face the music? We have all been called into the light; do not walk away.

Wisdom and understanding are the light. Who better to seek wisdom from than the creator of it? God created you, so why not be wise in his Word? "Then shalt thou understand the fear of the LORD, and find the knowledge of God." (Proverbs 2:5) Put on the eyes of the Lord. Make sense of everything that is happening around you. Don't just try to live out your own life in a world full of turmoil and destruction. Don't continue to follow the path of the wicked whose punishment is greater than death alone. Hear the Word of God, obey it and understand it. God is the light, the light that gives you life. Envision it in your life, in your children's life, and in your children's children life.

Sky Music

I just missed death like the car in front of the hearse.
Incubated, my spirit was premature at birth.
The pastor rinsed my soul but I got dirty again.
Stuck in the mud but now my roots don't blow in the wind.

Grounded, searching for new worlds that's already founded.
Free as a bird with wings that's bounded.
Surrounded by my enemies, the people have no inspiration.
Complain and at the same time complacent.

Chasing a dream that doesn't lead to the stars.
Gazing and grazing on a land that's not ours.
Faith is what you make it, but they'd rather believe in material.
Serial numbers identify individuals.

Residual citizens taught to forget they're imperial.
The power of bloodshed shall I drink from the cup.
How far will they push me before my mind just erupts?
Protected by the laws that don't protect for us.

Truth is in the history and those alive to tell it.
Some truth is erased for that intention to sell it.
Why does death come to those who fight hard to rebel it?
Who gives the heroes the heart to propel it?

January 23, 2009

I Am the Night

I am the night.
Look into my eyes you'll see the
    Stars burning bright
My face is round like the moon but a
    Glow more delight
There is evil in the shadows my
    Wings disperse the fright
If you could see through me then you
    Look into the light
…for I am the night.

                        April 2, 2009

Mind vs. Soul (Part II)

Now that I have your attention;
    You don't get to talk!
You've spoken enough for the both of us;
    Now I lead where we walk.
I wish you would say a word;
    Not a peep, not a sound!
If I didn't need you in my life;
    I'd cast you to the ground.
I don't need you to live;
    When you're gone I'll still be here.
Too bad I need you to grow old;
    Just like your grey hair.
Has it really been that long?
    You ain't tired of fighting me yet?
You were up, but now it's the 4th;
    You burned out quick like a jet
See this was a marathon run;
    You were good for a few miles.
Flowing well like the Mississippi;
    I'm more like the Nile.
The flashiness of your youth only blinded you from the truth.
Now you watch me seek wisdom, guidance, and reproof.
Nah, Nah…listen up,
    I'm not saying it's your fault.
Well not all of it…
    You couldn't possibly see your own fall.
Only when you're on the ground,
    That's how we get up again.
We can try this time together or…
    We can battle it to the end.
We can be a well oiled machine or…
    A self destructive force.
Just know that I hold the reigns;
    You're the bits in the horse!

                February 22, 2009

Confusion

We are gods because we are the children of God
Children are the descendents of their father
If we deny our father, we deny ourselves
Our Father is us and we are our Father

How then are we gods, even as God's children, being so full of sin?
In God there is no sin but the light of life
If we are free from sin then the light is in us
God is light so then God is in us
So when we die are we gods or angels,
    If the light was in us and we were saved?

                                      April 18, 2009

Wisdom

I walk through the darkness
    But I can see clear
The Lord gave me vision
    Eyes of man could not wear

              May 9, 2009

Conclusion

"This shall be written for the generation to come: and the people which shall be created shall praise the LORD."

Psalms 102:18

1. Out of the Darkness
   Step out of a sinful life towards the light of life.

2. Vision
   Begin by seeing yourself walking with God and a changed life.

3. Belief
   Believe God's word and that he can bring you out.

4. Love
   When you truly love something you follow it with your whole heart.

5. Forgiveness
   Ask God to forgive you for everything you've done. Forgive others for what they have done to you.

6. Change
   Turn away from your old lifestyle and begin a new one with God.

7. Commitment
   Commit to your new life with your whole heart and don't look back. Keep at it daily.

8. Sacrifice
   Forget about all the things you used to do and what you could do, if it jeopardizes your walk with God.

9. Obedience
   Obey the word of God.

10. Works
    Use your life for the will of God; let him use you.

11. Into the Light
    Understand your walk with God and teach it to others until he calls you home.

Concluding Prayer

Lord,

I am no longer in control. This vessel you have given me has been taken under siege and I have been sold into the slavery of sin. I cry out, but that which was mine is no longer under my command. Everything I want to be, everything true and righteous has fled from me and I am under the law of man. The more I attempt to break free, the more restraints they put on me to hold me back. I feel heavier than what I actually weigh because they force me to carry these chains with me everywhere I go. They deny my freedom even before I ask. What have I done or not done to bear this burden?

I've realized that they have actually been in control for a while now. Lord, I think it is time to remove these chains. How long shall I be a slave to unrighteousness? How long will you test my faith and my endurance? You are the one true God. I am not asking because you are not a man that you must answer to me. I pray to keep you near to me. I pray that you are my comforter for as long as I must endure. My strength is within and Lord, you are a strong tower in me. Lord, help me not to fail you. I do not cry out day and night because I do not want to trouble you with my pain and sufferings.

I do not blame you Lord, but I thank you. I thank you for my trouble. I thank you for these pains that help me realize I am in these chains and under the nature of sin. There are some who do not even know that they have been sold also. I thank you because I realize my faults and now I can be under the law of my Lord and Savior. I thank you because even though I have been sold to sin, I know also that I have been bought by you Lord. So I do not give way to my enemies by complaining or murmuring, but I put my whole heart in you Lord. In you Lord, I am free already.

No law can chain the mind except that which a man chooses, and I choose to obey you Lord. I choose to trust in you Lord. I choose to put all of my hope in knowing that you will deliver me.

I will not settle for anything less. Your promise of life is too great a gift to turn away, to turn back to that which was. These chains are an example to others. These chains are proof of the reality of sin, thus proving the reality of you Lord, your Holy Spirit, and Christ Jesus. The cries of the people are much more than my tears, much more than my pain, and much more than the need for my deliverance. Their minds have many shackles and some are clueless of the fact.

Lord, may your grace and mercy over-shadow us all from now into eternity. Free our spirit Lord. Free our mind Lord. In this land of bondage, Lord, free what cannot be bound by man but by sin that controls the nature of man. Free us in you. Bound us by your Word and chain us to your will and grace forever. That is what makes us free. Return us to the garden to be with you always: forever in your presence; forever in your company; forever in your companionship.

All praise, honor, and glory to you Father, our Lord God, that through Jesus Christ has given us a Light in the darkness and freedom from restraints. Blessed be your name for all times. May you be high and lifted up. May my soul rejoice and be glad the day I am with you. And may our love continue forever. I thank you for your Word, and for sharing your wisdom, and for showing your awesome power and glory. We love and praise you forever, always.

Amen.

Appendix

Out of the Darkness
1. I John 2:16
2. Job 28:28
3. Job 33:24

Vision
1. Daniel 10:14
2. Proverbs 1:7
3. Matthew 6:21
4. Matthew 6:22-23
5. I Timothy 6:10
6. II Timothy 3:1-7

Belief
1. John 1:1-5
2. Hebrews 11:1
3. II Corinthians 5:7
4. Romans 10:17
5. Romans 10:9-10
6. John 4:24
7. I John 3:8
8. John 3:16

Love
1. *I Corinthians 13:4-8 (NCV)
2. Romans 5:8
3. *I Corinthians 13:13 (NCV)

Forgiveness
1. *Psalm 130:3-4 (NIV)
2. Psalm 78:38
3. Luke 7:47
4. Ephesians 4:32
5. Ezekiel 18:30-32

Change
1. Luke 9:23
2. Malachi 3:6
3. Luke 15:7
4. Luke 13:3
5. II Corinthians 7:10
6. Acts 2:38
7. Mark 16:16

Commitment
1. II Chronicles 15:2
2. II Chronicles 16:9
3. Matthew 7:8-9
4. Matthew 7:23
5. II Chronicles 26:5

Sacrifice
1. Proverbs 24:16
2. Job 2:10
3. Proverbs 3:11-12

Obedience
1. I Samuel 15:22
2. Psalms 119:2
3. Matthew 6:24
4. Matthew 4:4
5. Romans 6:23

Works
1. I Corinthians 12:4-6
2. I Corinthians 12:20
3. Matthew 16:27
4. James 2:26

Into the Light
1. I John 1:5-7
2. John 3:19-21
3. Proverbs 2:5

* Unless otherwise noted verses are quoted from KJV.

Study Material

*"For to be carnally minded is death;
but to be spiritually minded is life and peace.*

Romans 8:6

Foreigners on Earth

Death

We all must die. This is an understood fact of life. Humans and animals, and plants alike must die one day. The flesh which embodies our spirit one day will perish. But we have another body, which is the spirit. The natural body decays and is buried, but the spiritual body never dies.

> I Corinthians 15:35-44 *Natural Body vs. Spiritual Body*
> Isaiah 25:8 *Victory over Death*
> Hosea 13:14 *Victory over Death*

Resurrection

First we die, as Jesus did. Then we are resurrected, as Jesus was. To go any further in your walk with God, your faith in Christ, and your belief in the Bible, you must believe that Jesus died and was resurrected if you can't believe that then your faith is in vain. Jesus died, was raised and now sits on the throne at the right hand.

> I Corinthians 15:12-19 *Death and Resurrection*
> Hebrews 12:2 *Jesus Is With God*

Heavenly Home

Once you've accepted death and resurrection, you have to believe that there is a place for you in heaven. If we believe and follow God's commandments, we will reside there. We are only on earth temporarily. This earth will pass away and there will be a new heaven and new earth. Everything we do here on earth is to prepare for our home in heaven.

> John 14:1-6 *A Place in Heaven*

Revelation 21:1-4 *New Heaven and New Earth*
Hebrews 13:14 *Seek Heaven*
II Corinthians 5:1-6 *Home In Heaven*

Earthly Home

Sometimes I get the feeling I don't belong here on earth. That's right! We don't belong here but in heaven. That doesn't mean go commit suicide. God has a purpose for each one of us here on earth. Even before the world began, God had a plan. No one knows the thoughts of God except the Spirit of God. When we receive the Spirit of God only then can we know what God has given us. We speak about those things through the Spirit and not through human wisdom, and unless we have the mind of Christ how can we be instructed by Christ. Receive the mind of Christ, follow his Word, and be received into heaven. Our real home.

Hebrews 11:13 *Pilgrims on Earth*
I Corinthians 2 *Spirit of God and Wisdom of God*
I Peter 2:11 *Strangers and Pilgrims*

Staying Put

Obedience

People make plans for their lives: work they want to do, houses they want to live in, and where they want to live. Sometimes they pray about it, sometimes they don't. The people of Judah asked Jeremiah to ask God what they should do. God warned them to stay put; that if they left Judah terrible things would happen and they would die. They had the luxury of knowing what would happen if they left, and they still disobeyed. God knows our future. If we obey him, he will watch over us. He is patient with us; we should be patient and let God do his work.

Jeremiah 42 *God Advises Jeremiah*

Disobedience

The people of Judah feared the power of man more than they feared the power of God. Even though they knew and understood God's answer, they did not stay in Judah. They lacked faith and a lack of faith causes disobedience. The human mind likes to rationalize situations. God would rather we not think and just listen because he already has a plan of escape for us. If we fear God, we tend to be more obedient. Since the human mind can only fear what it sees, God usually has to put trouble in our life in order for us to fear and depend on him.

Jeremiah 43:2-7 *Judah Disobeys*

Consequences

There are consequences for being obedient or disobedient. God told the people of Judah either stay and live or go and die. Simple instructions and they still left. As a result, the people of Judah ran towards war, death, and terrible diseases. The same goes for us. By not obeying, we can actually be running towards trouble. If we obey, however, God keeps us in his wall of protection safe from harm. It is much safer to obey than to disobey, don't you think? The people of Judah didn't think so and they died as a result. Fear God, the one and only creator and destroyer of our souls. Learn to be patient and obey.

Jeremiah 44:11-14 *Consequences for Judah*

Other Verses

Genesis 37-39 *Joseph in Egypt*
Exodus 14 *God Delivers Israel*

Army of God
Part I

Enlisting

Qualifications:

To qualify, God wants you to believe in your heart that he is, repent for your sins and turn to him and he will begin his work in you. He has to be able to use you.

> Romans 10:9-10 *Confess Jesus Is Lord*
> Acts 2:38 *Repent and be Baptized*

Fit for the job:

Now that your heart is open to God, he has to know how you will respond when you are attacked so he will test you. Nobody goes out to fight a war without first being trained. God has to test your faith.

> Genesis 3:6 *Adam Tested*
> Genesis 22:1-12 *Abraham Tested*
> Job 1:8 *Satan Permitted to Test Job*
> Luke 4:1-13 *Jesus Tested*

Loyalty:

You have been tested and now deemed fit for the work of God. Now you must remain loyal to him. There is a division between the world and God and you must continue to stand strong on God's side: even if your family does not, friends do not, or co-workers do not. God trusts you to perform well in your position. Trust that he has provided you with the proper training.

Proverbs 3:5-6 *Trust In God*
Matthew 6:24 *Cannot Serve Two Masters*
Matthew 16:24 *Deny Yourself*
Luke 12:51-53 *Choosing Sides*
I Corinthians 10:21 *Choosing Sides*
I Peter 2:9 *Set Apart*

Equipped

Equipment:

1. Belt of Truth
2. Breastplate of Righteousness
3. Footgear- fitted to be ready to spread the Good News
4. Shield of Faith
5. Helmet of Salvation
6. Sword of the Spirit- The Word of God

Remember this is a war and I hope you did not sign up thinking you could get a desk job. The sword is your only weapon and the only physical thing in your armory. You have to learn how to use it or your other protective gear might fail. Read the manual over and over until it is embedded in your heart.

Ephesians 6:10 -18 *Armor of God*

Educate:

In your manual, you will find that your sword can decipher between friend and foe. Trust in the Word. There are traits that give the enemy away. You will be attacked. You were in the war before you knew it and now that you have enlisted on God's side, you are going to be attacked first. The enemy uses this strategy to prevent further recruitment.

Galatians 5:19-21 *Traits of the Enemy*

Galatians 5:22-25 *Traits of an Ally*
I Timothy 6:10 *Origin of the Enemy*
II Timothy 3:1-7 *What to Expect*
I John 3:16-17 *Outcome of the War*
I John 4:1 *Knowing Who is On Your Side*
II Corinthians 10:3-6 *Warfare*

Seal of the Spirit:

Believe it or not, you were given the 'Seal of the Spirit' the day you enlisted. This emblem identifies you as a member in the Army of God. There are no ranks, just 'The Seal'. This seal will always identify you and every good and evil spirit will recognize it. Do not be afraid. You have your equipment and are educated, prepared, and trained. Identify yourself with others wearing 'The Seal' so you do not have to fight alone.

Daniel 10:12 *Enlistment Day*
Ephesians 1:13 *Seal of the Promise*
Ephesians 4:4-6 *One Body in Christ*
Philippians 1:6 *Eternally Associated*
II Timothy 1:7 *Power, Love, and Sound Mind*

Army of God
Part II: Desert Training

The desert is a safe haven with God's protection and a place for spiritual strengthening.

Desert Briefing

What you will learn:
1) How to become totally dependent on god
2) Various ways to strengthen your spirit
3) Various ways Satan attacks us
4) How to use training in everyday life

What you will experience:
1) Physical Weakness
2) Spiritual Weakness
3) Spiritual Strength

Training

Dependency:

    The desert represents times of trouble. Trouble causes panic, weariness, worry, and pain. God looks for us to become On-Him-Dependent and not self-dependent. Not relying on God can keep you in the desert longer. You must pass the first lesson to proceed through the rest of your training.
    Trouble can also cause us to be angry, jealous, or envious because we look at the comfort of others and desire what they have. As a result, we tend to ask God, "Why, why?" or blame Him for our trouble. Learn to trust that God provides and if you do not have it then you probably don't need it.

Exodus 14:10-14 *Israel before the Red Sea*
Exodus 16:1-11 *God Provides*
Exodus 17:1-7 *Testing God*
Numbers 14 *Consequences of Blaming God*
Proverbs 3:5-6 *Trusting God*
Proverbs 3:11-12 *Correction*

Spiritual Strength:

The desert is designed to purify your spirit. Like a fire purifies gold, the purpose is for you to come out better than before. Naturally, the flesh (physical-self) would rather not be tested. It desires the easy, "free" life, but life is neither easy nor free. The purpose is to break down the flesh and build up the spirit.

Ways to strengthen the spirit:

Prayer – builds a personal relationship with God and dependency on Him
Reading – helps understand what is required of your spirit
Fasting – prepares your spirit for desert situations
Fellowship – is how you apply training

Signs of Spiritual Strength: patience, faithfulness, and endurance

Matthew 4:1-11 *Knowing the Word*
Matthew 5:3-11 *Rewards of Spiritual Strength*
Matthew 7:7-8 *Spiritual Wisdom*
Galatians 6:7-8 *Reap What You Sow*

Spiritual Attacks:

In the desert, you will be physically weak. This is a perfect time for the enemy to attack. If you've trained your spirit well these attacks will not be hard for you to handle. You must be rooted in your faith. While the flesh is weak, Satan will attack you hoping to break your spirit and get you back in the flesh, the exact opposite of the purpose of being in the desert. This is why you must learn dependency first.

Ways you will be attacked: Lust, Pride, Envy, Jealousy, Greed, Fear, Ambition, Anger, Hatred, Witchcraft, and Disobedience. He can use all or one and twist and turn them every which way to get you to break or turn from God just for an instant. The more you turn, the less of a threat and a witness you are which makes you God's enemy.

Genesis 3:1-6 *Satan Tests Eve*
Exodus 7:1-12 *Imitation of Miracles*
Job 1, 2 *Satan Tests Job*
Matthew 4:1-11 *Satan Tests Jesus*
II Corinthians 2:11 *Not Ignorant*
II Timothy 1:7 *Fear from Satan*
I John 2:16-17 *World vs. God's Will*

Applications in Life:

1) Depend fully on the Lord
2) Practice building spiritual strength daily
3) Be aware of the attacks in your life
4) Fight back in spirit and teach others

Spiritually Strong Examples

Genesis 22:1-17 *Abraham offers Isaac*
Joshua 6 *Joshua at Jericho*
Judges 7 *Gideon's Army*
I Samuel 17 *David vs. Goliath*
Daniel 3 *Shadrach, Meshach, & Abednego*
Revelation 12 *The Women and the Dragon*

Questions:

What "Spiritual Desert" are you in?
Have you looked to God first?

Growing Your Seed

Our natural bodies are a casing or cover for our spiritual bodies. Our spiritual bodies are like a seed that must be buried and watered to grow. If you compare your spiritual body to the seed of a fruit, you can infer that it has not yet taken its shape until it has grown and the casing or flesh has been removed. After the flesh has died, the spirit will take the form of what God has made it to be. We are all gardeners and have been given the responsibility of growing our seed properly.

Process of Growth

1) Sow
2) Water
3) Light
4) Metamorphosis
5) Growth
6) Fruit

Sow

How you sow your seed (spirit), determines if it will bear fruit. Where you sow your seed, determines the result of the fruit. What you sow, determines what you will reap.

Psalm 126:5 *Reaping Joy*
Proverbs 11:18 *Sowing Righteousness*
Matthew 5:3-11 *What to Sow*
Mark 4:3-8, 14-20 *Where to Sow*
Galatians 6:7-8 *Sowing & Reaping in Spirit*
I Corinthians 15:42-44 *How to Sow Your Seed*
II Corinthians 9:6 *Reap As Much As You Sow*

Water

Water is life. Without water we would not exist. A seed needs water to grow and the miracle of life begins with water. A seed that does not receive water will not grow and dies. The spirit is a seed and it too must be watered. Allowing God's Spirit into yours is how you water your spirit. Praise, worship, prayer, fasting, and studying the Word is how you allow God's Spirit in.

Ways to water your spirit:
I Chronicles 16:22 *Seek the Lord*
Psalm 35:13 *Humble Yourself with Fasting*
Psalm 100:2 *Serve with Gladness*
John 4:24 *Worship in Spirit and Truth*
I Thessalonians 5:17 *Pray without Ceasing*
Hebrews 13:15 *Praise Him Continually*

Light

Light causes growth. Without light, your seed cannot grow either. The sun is the source of light for the natural seed. The Word of God and the Son, which is Jesus Christ, is the source of light for the spiritual seed. The Light is knowledge, wisdom, and understanding. If your spirit cannot comprehend, it cannot grow.

Psalm 19:8 *Enlightening the Eyes*
Psalm 119:130 *The Word Gives Light*
Proverbs 9:10 *Beginning of Knowledge*
John 1:1-4 *Word of God*
John 8:12 *Jesus is Light of the World*

Metamorphosis

Metamorphosis means to change in form. There is no way you can sow a seed in good ground, water it, and give it light and it not change forms. The same applies for your spirit; there will be a change in you. First, a seed must die in order to become something new, its old form will pass away. The flesh must die in order for the spirit to live. Baptism is how we symbolically bury the flesh and sow the seed. Rising up out of the water is symbolic for the growth and life of the spirit. Metamorphosis for your spirit occurs before the water, under the water, and after the water.

John 3:5-8 *Born Again*
John 12:24 *If It Dies*
I Corinthians 15:31 *Die Daily*
I Corinthians 15:49-50 *Earthly Image & Heavenly Image*
I Peter 1:23 *Born of Incorruptible Seed*

Growth

After the seed has taken its new form, it grows into a body that is able to produce fruit. The apple grows from a tree and the grape from a vine. The spirit grows after taking the form of the Holy Spirit, which works in us. Having the Spirit of God allows us to bear fruit that produces eternal life.

How to grow and bear fruit:

James 1:22-27 *Be Doers of the Word*

Fruit

Once a seed has grown into its new body, it can now bear fruit. Hearing and doing the Word bears fruit for your spirit. You can tell when the Holy Spirit has sown a seed in a person's spirit by the fruit they bear.

Fruits of the Spirit:
Mark 4:30-32 *Little Seed Bears Much Fruit*
Galatians 5:22-26 *Fruits of the Spirit*
Hebrews 12:11 *Fruit of Righteousness*

"…it is not the healthy who need a doctor, but the sick."

Matthew 9:12

CPSIA information can be obtained at www.ICGtesting.com
Printed in the USA
LVOW11s1255050814

397587LV00001B/10/P